D0573021

MY FIRST SPORTS

Swimming

by Anne Wendorff

BELLWETHER MEDIA • MINNEAPOLIS, MN

Note to Librarians, Teachers, and Parents:

Blastoff! Readers are carefully developed by literacy experts and combine standards-based content with developmentally appropriate text.

Level 1 provides the most support through repetition of high-frequency words, light text, predictable sentence patterns, and strong visual support.

Level 2 offers early readers a bit more challenge through varied simple sentences, increased text load, and less repetition of high-frequency words.

Level 3 advances early-fluent readers toward fluency through increased text and concept load, less reliance on visuals, longer sentences, and more literary language.

Level 4 builds reading stamina by providing more text per page, increased use of punctuation, greater variation in sentence patterns, and increasingly challenging vocabulary.

Level 5 encourages children to move from "learning to read" to "reading to learn" by providing even more text, varied writing styles, and less familiar topics.

Whichever book is right for your reader, Blastoff! Readers are the perfect books to build confidence and encourage a love of reading that will last a lifetime!

48225675 3/12

This edition first published in 2010 by Bellwether Media, Inc.

No part of this publication may be reproduced in whole or in part without written permission of the publisher. For information regarding permission, write to Bellwether Media, Inc., Attention: Permissions Department, Post Office Box 19349, Minneapolis, MN 55419.

Library of Congress Cataloging-in-Publication Data
Wendorff, Anne.
  Swimming / by Anne Wendorff.
     p. cm. – (Blastoff! readers. My first sports)
  Includes bibliographical references and index.
  Summary: "Simple text and full color photographs introduce beginning readers to the sport of swimming. Developed by literacy experts for students in grades two through five"–Provided by publisher.
  ISBN 978-1-60014-326-7 (hardcover : alk. paper)
  1. Swimming–Juvenile literature. I. Title.

GV837.6.W46 2009
797.2'1–dc22
                                        2009008182

Contents

What Is Swimming?

Swimming is the act of moving through water using your arms and legs. People have been swimming for a very long time. The sport of swimming, however, was created in England.

The first swimming pools for racing were built in the early 1800s. The first known swim **meets** took place at these pools in the 1830s.

At first, there were only a few short races during swim meets. Swimmers used the **breaststroke** and the **front crawl** in these races.

As the sport grew, swimmers began competing in longer races and creating more **strokes**. In 1912, swimming became a sport in the **Olympics**.

The Basic Rules of Swimming

Olympic-size pools are 50 meters (164 feet) long. There are also pools that are 23 meters (75 feet) long. All pools have six to eight **lanes**. Floating **lane lines** separate the lanes.

starting block

A **starting block** is at one end of each lane. Swimmers dive off starting blocks into the pool at the beginning of each race.

Swimmers are timed during their races. The swimmer with the fastest time is the winner of the race. In some races, swimmers compete across short distances such as 50 meters (164 feet) and 100 meters (328 feet). Swimmers also race across long distances such as 1,500 meters (4,921 feet).

Swimmers can race alone or with a team. A team race is called a relay.

Swimmers use four strokes to move through the water. The four strokes are **freestyle**, **backstroke**, breaststroke, and **butterfly**.

Each stroke uses different muscles and movements to push swimmers forward. Swimmers often use a strong dolphin kick or a flutter kick to move through the water. A swimmer's legs move together in a dolphin kick. They move separately in a flutter kick.

Swimmers turn around at the end of their lanes in different ways. They make a **flip turn** when they are swimming freestyle or using the backstroke.

14

Swimmers use a different way to turn when swimming the breaststroke or the butterfly. They must touch the end of the pool with both hands before turning around.

Swimming Equipment

Swimmers use equipment to help them move quickly through the water. Swimsuits are lightweight and tight. A loose swimsuit would slow a swimmer down in the water.

Swimmers also wear **swim caps** and **goggles**. Swim caps hold back hair. Goggles allow swimmers to see underwater. Being able to see underwater lets swimmers stay in their lanes. They also know when they reach the end of the pool.

Swimming Today

Today, swimmers practice and compete with local **swim clubs**. Swimmers are ranked in each event by their fastest times. The fastest swimmers in the United States compete with the U.S. National Team. They race in meets around the world and in the Olympics.

The Olympics is the sport's biggest event. American Michael Phelps proved he was one of the world's fastest swimmers during the 2008 Olympics.

He learned the sport at a local swim club. Phelps and other top swimmers continue to change the sport as they find faster ways to move through the water!

! fun fact

Michael Phelps won eight gold medals at the 2008 Olympics.

Glossary

backstroke—a swimming stroke; swimmers lie on their backs and use one arm at a time to move forward.

breaststroke—a swimming stroke; swimmers lie facedown and use both arms at the same time underwater to pull themselves forward.

butterfly—a swimming stroke; swimmers lie facedown and bring both arms up out of the water, thrust them forward, and draw them back underwater while performing a dolphin kick.

flip turn—an underwater somersault that turns a swimmer around

freestyle—a stroke where swimmers choose how they want to swim; the front crawl is the fastest freestyle stroke.

front crawl—a swimming stroke that is often used in freestyle races

goggles—a piece of swimming equipment used to keep water out of swimmers' eyes

lane—a marked path that swimmers use in a race

lane line—floating markers that create swimming lanes in a pool

meet—a swimming competition

Olympics—a worldwide sporting event held every four years

starting block—a raised surface that swimmers dive off of at the start of a race

stroke—the way a swimmer moves through the water; the four swimming strokes are freestyle, breaststroke, backstroke, and butterfly.

swim cap—a cap that covers a swimmer's head and prevents hair from getting in a swimmer's eyes

swim club—a group of swimmers and coaches who practice together

To Learn More

AT THE LIBRARY
Kehm, Greg. *Olympic Swimming and Diving*.
New York, N.Y.: Rosen, 2007.

Kessler, Leonard. *Last One in Is a Rotten Egg*.
New York, N.Y.: HarperCollins, 1999.

Wallace, Karen. *I Can Swim*. New York, N.Y.:
DK Publishing, 2004.

ON THE WEB
Learning more about swimming
is as easy as 1, 2, 3.

1. Go to www.factsurfer.com.

2. Enter "swimming" into the search box.

3. Click the "Surf" button and you will see a list of
   related Web sites.

With factsurfer.com, finding more information is just a
click away.

Index